Sumptuous Sauces

IN THE MICROWAVE